Hello!
I am a
polar bear.

I0108787

The average lifespan of a polar bear is around 20 to 30 years.

But some of us have lived more than 35 years.

Polar bears are from a place called the Arctic.

That is near the north pole.

Polar bears are the largest bear in the world.

Polar bears mostly eat seals.

They also eat whales, fish, and other small mammals.

I can eat up to 88 pounds (40 kilograms) of meat in one meal.

Polar bears have a great sense of smell.

I will wait hours if I need to.

Polar bears are patient hunters and will wait near a seal's breathing hole in the ice.

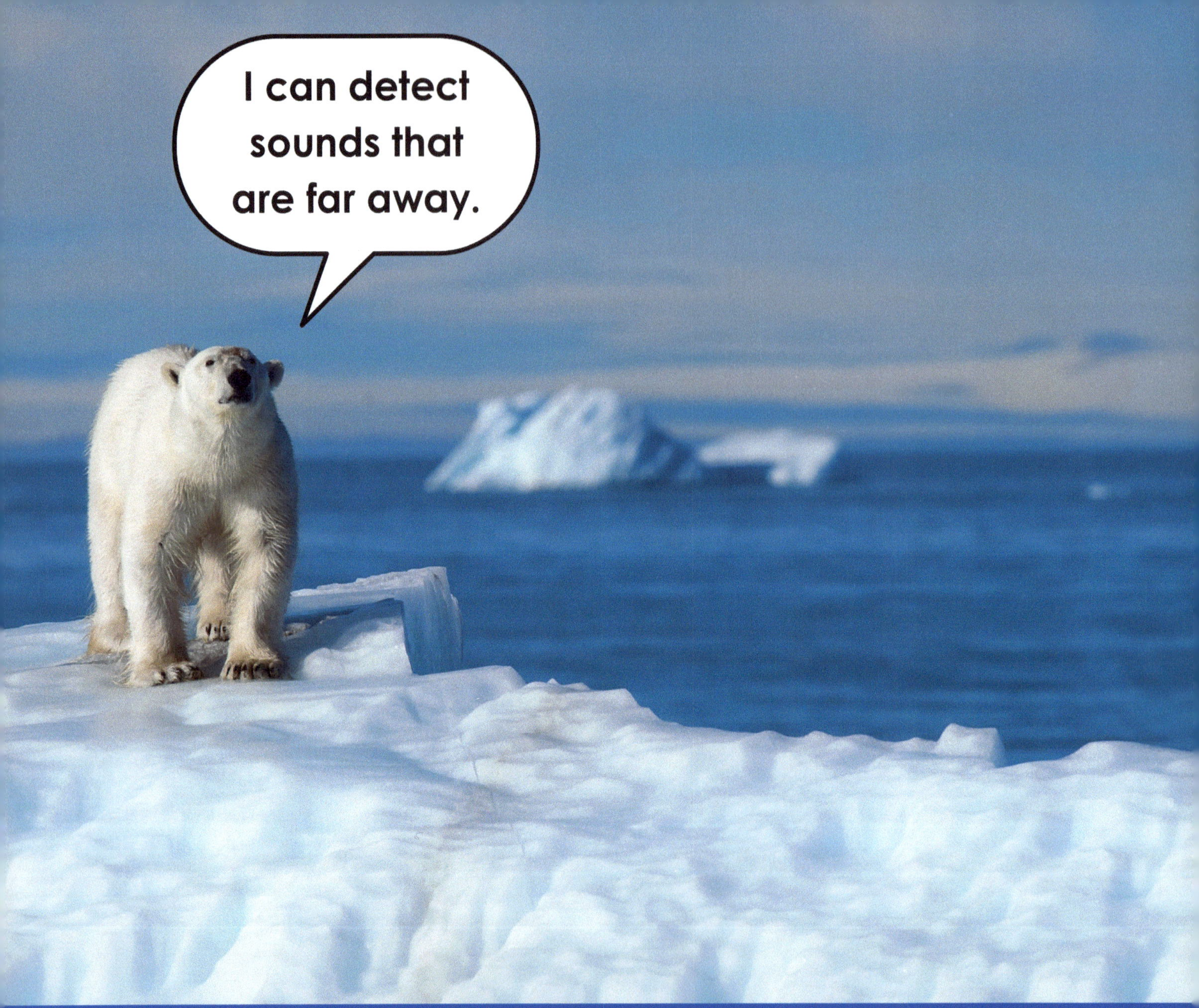

They have a strong sense of hearing.

Polar bears have small ears that help prevent heat loss.

Polar bears are at the top of the Arctic food chain.

I have no natural predators.

Polar bears can go months without eating during the summer when food is scarce.

Polar bears can close their nostrils.

This helps me keep water out while swimming.

They can dive underwater to catch fish and other marine animals.

Polar bears have a thick, powerful neck that helps them break through ice to breathe.

They are excellent swimmers and can swim long distances.

I have webbed feet that help me paddle through the water.

Polar bears are good climbers and can climb on icebergs and rocky cliffs.

I can grip the ice with my paws.

Polar bears have a thick layer of fur on the bottom of their paws.

Polar bears have a white fur coat but...

...their skin is actually black.

I blend in with the snow and ice.
My skin helps me absorb heat from the sun.

Polar bears have strong jaws and sharp teeth to catch and eat their prey.

I can stay warm in freezing weather.

They have a thick layer of fat called blubber.

Polar bears can run 40 miles (64km) per hour .

When I stand up, I want to show you I'm in charge.

Me too.

Polar bears use noises, their scent, body language, and movement to communicate.

Polar bears make dens by creating a tunnel in the snow and ice.

The nickname for polar bears is "King of the Arctic".

Baby bears are called "cubs".

Cubs stay with their mother for about two and a half years.

We will learn to be independent.

Polar bears are solitary animals.

... and more

Hello parents!

scan here

Visit us to find out about new releases and *FREE* offers. We'll let you know when we have a new release coming out and how you can get it for FREE.
And you can cast your vote for what book we make next!

ActiveBrainsBooks.com

or visit here

---

scan here

Let us know what you think. As an independent publisher, your honest reviews mean a lot to us and our business. We'd love to hear from you!

amazon.com/review/create-review/

or visit here

FOLLOW US on Amazon.

amazon.com/author/activebrainsbooks

ACTIVE BRAINS

ActiveBrainsBooks.com

www.ingramcontent.com/pod-product-compliance
Lightning Source LLC
Chambersburg PA
CBHW042057040426
42447CB00003B/255

9 781957 337586